MEET
Buffy Sainte-Marie

SCHOLASTIC CANADA BIOGRAPHY

ELIZABETH MACLEOD

ILLUSTRATED BY
MIKE DEAS

Scholastic Canada Ltd.
Toronto New York London Auckland Sydney
Mexico City New Delhi Hong Kong Buenos Aires

As Buffy Sainte-Marie sang, she could feel the audience listening carefully. People in the crowded Toronto coffee house hung on every word of her song. It explained how Indigenous Peoples' children, cultures and lands had been taken from them.

Buffy loved singing and writing songs. And she saw how her music could connect with people, and teach and inspire them.

Perhaps Buffy could use her songs to make the world better for everyone.

Beverly "Buffy" Sainte-Marie does not know for sure when or where she was born. It was likely in the early 1940s on the Piapot First Nation reserve, in the Qu'Appelle Valley, Saskatchewan.

Up until the 1980s, many Indigenous children were taken from their families and adopted out to White people. This was one of the Canadian government systems that knowingly hurt Indigenous Peoples. Families were broken up, and children lost their parents, languages, cultures and communities.

Who Buffy's birth parents were isn't known for certain either. She was adopted as a baby by Albert and Winifred Sainte-Marie and grew up in the northeastern United States. Buffy's mom was part Mi'kmaq, a First Nation in eastern Canada and the northeastern United States.

Buffy's mom told her she was sorry she didn't know anything about Indigenous cultures, neither hers nor Buffy's. But she also told Buffy that, when she grew up, she could find out all kinds of things on her own, including learning about Indigenous cultures. And that's what Buffy did.

5

There were bullies in Buffy's family and in the neighbourhood. She played by herself a lot. Her best friends were animals and her imagination.

Buffy loved playing the piano. She could play a tune after hearing it once. She made up her own songs from an early age.

Buffy didn't learn music by lessons or by reading it. She learned "by ear," by listening.

She has a kind of dyslexia that makes it hard for her to read music.

When Buffy was sixteen, she got her first guitar and taught herself how to play it. She didn't know the standard tuning most people use, so she just made up her own.

7

In 1959, Buffy became the first person in her family to go to university. She studied philosophy and trained to be a teacher.

There were no other Indigenous students in her classes. But in the summer, she met members of the National Indian Youth Council in Washington, D.C. Buffy was inspired by the ways they were working to protect their lands and cultures.

While at university, Buffy kept creating songs. She played them for the women in her dormitory. Next, she began playing her songs in small music clubs, and then bigger and bigger ones.

After Buffy graduated from university, she continued performing. It wasn't long before she was playing music full-time. But her career was about to change completely.

In 1962, Buffy was flying to Toronto to play a show. At the airport she saw a group of wounded American soldiers. They had been fighting in Vietnam, a country in Southeast Asia. What Buffy saw saddened and horrified her.

When she arrived at the coffee house, Buffy sat down and wrote "Universal Soldier." This antiwar song was on her first album, *It's My Way*. Buffy sang about how everyone had a responsibility to try to stop wars. It became a famous protest anthem.

In 1965, Buffy released her second album, *Many a Mile*. It included the song "Until It's Time for You to Go." This love song was immediately a big hit. It has been recorded by more than 200 singers, including Barbra Streisand and Elvis Presley, and it was played by the Boston Pops Orchestra.

Buffy's success made her famous. She was a guest on talk shows, variety shows and even on a game show.

In 1968, Buffy was asked to take a lead role in an episode of *The Virginian*, a ninety-minute television drama.

Buffy made sure her role was a positive reflection of an Indigenous character. Buffy had seen how Indigenous roles were depicted on TV and in movies. Often they were written as lazy, portrayed as thieves or villains who were played by non-Indigenous actors wearing bad wigs and makeup.

The producers thought there weren't enough professional Indigenous actors for all the parts. But Buffy knew lots of people at the Indian Actors' Workshop in Hollywood. She arranged that they play all the characters.

This was the first production that used Indigenous actors for all the Indigenous roles. Buffy proved that it was possible for shows to be more diverse, and that diversity made them better.

13

With the money Buffy earned from her music, she started the Nihewan Foundation for Native American Education in 1969.

Buffy worried about how few Indigenous teens went to university. So her foundation created scholarships for Indigenous high school graduates to help pay for university. The group encouraged younger students to prepare for it.

For years Buffy travelled the world, spending time in great cities and also Indigenous communities in Europe and Asia. She saw how people in media and education often disrespected Indigenous Peoples. As a teacher and an entertainer, she wanted to give the whole world a better understanding about the past, present and future contributions of Indigenous Peoples.

Buffy was winning awards for her songs and had many fans around the world. But it suddenly became hard for people to listen to her music. She was rarely played on U.S. radio in the 1970s.

That was because of powerful people who were connected to the United States government. They didn't like how Buffy supported the rights of Indigenous Peoples protecting the land. Radio stations were told not to play her songs.

But that didn't stop her from making music.

In 1976, Buffy combined Indigenous singing with pop music, calling it powwow rock. She wrote a song called "Starwalker," a celebration of Indigenous Peoples and their accomplishments.

"Starwalker" was on Buffy's album *Sweet America*. She dedicated the album to the American Indian Movement. This group works to end poverty and discrimination, and champions Indigenous rights.

Between 1975 and 1981, Buffy appeared on *Sesame Street*. She wanted to show viewers that Indigenous Peoples are their neighbours and friends.

Sharing parts of Indigenous cultures was important to Buffy.
She taught the Count how to count in nêhiyawêwin (Cree).

She played the mouthbow. It's a handmade instrument made with a curved, flexible stick and a string stretched between its ends.

Buffy also breastfed her son, Cody, on the show. That made her the first person to breastfeed on national television.

Buffy liked acting, but she was still a songwriter. When she was asked to co-write a song for the film *An Officer and a Gentleman*, she already had a melody in mind. "Up Where We Belong" was a number-one hit around the world.

In 1983, the song won Buffy an Academy Award, or Oscar, the highest honour in the movie industry.

Music wasn't the only way Buffy expressed her creativity. In 1984, she began using her computer to make art. At that time there weren't very many artists working this way.

Many of Buffy's huge, colourful paintings now hang in art galleries and museums. Her visual art shows how the past can be connected to the future with new technologies.

Buffy also loves using new music technology. Her 1969 album *Illuminations* was one of the first to include electronic vocals. It was also the first album recorded using an early form of surround sound.

In 1991, Buffy created much of her album *Coincidence and Likely Stories* using a computer at her home recording studio. Then she sent it to her record producer using the internet. This was groundbreaking at the time.

Buffy realized she could use computers for something even greater — bringing kids together. In 1996, she started the Cradleboard Teaching Project. Using online interactive multimedia, students studied science, government and other subjects through Indigenous eyes. The project also connected classes around the world to create cross-cultural friendships and understanding.

In November 2012, four women in Saskatchewan founded the group Idle No More to work for Indigenous rights. Buffy took part in their protests and posted about them on social media.

This grassroots organization brings together Indigenous and non-Indigenous people. It connects those living in cities and on remote reserves. Idle No More works to make things fairer and to protect the land, sky and water. No wonder Buffy spoke at their rallies!

In 2015, Buffy recorded *Power in the Blood*. This album of rock, protest and love songs talks about Indigenous rights, decolonization and stopping war.

It won the Polaris Music Prize for Best Canadian Album. It also won Juno Awards for Best Aboriginal Album and Best Contemporary Roots Album. That same year, Buffy won the Spirit of Americana/Free Speech in Music Award. She was the first non-American winner.

Buffy still performs around the world. Some of her concerts raise money for various charities.

Playing shows is a lot of work, but at each concert, Buffy makes time to connect with her fans. Whether she's singing her classic songs or her new ones, every concert is a chance to celebrate music. Buffy encourages people to think about ways they can make the world a better place.

When Buffy is not playing a concert or festival, she really likes being with her cats, dogs, goats and horses — all shelter animals who needed a home. She has lived on a farm in Hawai'i since 1966.

Animals mean a lot to Buffy. In 2020, she wrote a children's book called *Hey Little Rockabye*. It encourages people to adopt rescue pets. The book also raises money for Humane Canada, an organization that cares for animals.

Whether it's a love song or protest song, Buffy is known around the world for her music. Her songs talk about putting an end to war, standing up for human rights, celebrating Indigenous cultures and protecting the Earth.

Using the power of positivity, Buffy shares her messages with her songs and through art, education and the organizations she supports. Buffy teaches that we can all work together to help make the world a better place.

Buffy Sainte-Marie's Life

Early 1940s	Beverly Sainte-Marie is born, likely on the Piapot First Nation in the Qu'Appelle Valley, Saskatchewan. She is adopted by Albert and Winifred Sainte-Marie.
Late 1950s	Beverly is given the nickname Buffy while in high school.
1959	Buffy begins studying at the University of Massachusetts Amherst, going on to earn degrees in education and Oriental philosophy.
1963	Buffy releases her song "Universal Soldier" from her first album, *It's My Way!*
1969	Buffy starts the Nihewan Foundation for Native American Education.
1975	Buffy appears regularly on *Sesame Street* until 1981.
1983	Buffy becomes the first Indigenous person to win an Oscar. It is for a song she co-wrote called "Up Where We Belong."
1997	Buffy founds the Cradleboard Teaching Project.
1997	Buffy is named an Officer of the Order of Canada. She becomes a Companion of the Order of Canada in 2019.
2009	Buffy wins a Juno Award for Aboriginal Recording of the Year for *Running for the Drum*.
2010	Buffy wins the Governor General's Performing Arts Award.

CANADA POST RELEASED THIS STAMP IN 2021.

BUFFY ONSTAGE AT THE FAMOUS NEWPORT FOLK FESTIVAL IN 1967.

2015   Buffy's album *Power in the Blood* wins the Polaris Music Prize.

Buffy wins the Spirit of Americana/Free Speech in Music Award.

2016   Buffy wins Juno Awards for Aboriginal Album of the Year and Contemporary Roots Album of the Year for *Power in the Blood*.

2018   Buffy wins Indigenous Music Awards for Best Folk Album for *Medicine Songs* and Best Video for "The War Racket."

Buffy wins the Juno Award for Indigenous Music Album of the Year for *Medicine Songs*.

2020   Buffy publishes her first children's book, *Hey Little Rockabye*.

Buffy wins a Polaris Heritage Prize, honouring great Canadian albums of the past, for *It's My Way!*

2021   Buffy is named a Pillar of the new Academy Awards Museum in Los Angeles, California. Her Oscar is on display there.

2022   Buffy publishes a picture book, *Still This Love Goes On,* and a chapter book, *Tapwe and the Magic Hat*, which is written in both English and nêhiyawêwin.

BUFFY AT AN IDLE NO MORE RALLY ON THE NATIONAL DAY OF PROTEST, JANUARY 27, 2013.

BUFFY SINGS "POWER IN THE BLOOD" AT THE 2015 POLARIS MUSIC PRIZE GALA.

*MJ and bob dedicate this to Zoe and Genevieve, women with a passion
for justice who yearn for a world where all know dignity.*
— E.M.

For future music creatives.
— M.D.

Thanks as ever to my wonderful editor, Erin O'Connor. I know this book was a labour of love for
her and I loved working on it with her. She really makes all the text sing! Mike Deas, illustrations
just get better and better — thanks especially for all the cats! I also deeply appreciate the work of
designer Andrea Casault, copy editor Erin Haggett and everyone at Scholastic Canada.

Very special thanks to Buffy Sainte-Marie for her time and willingness to answer my questions.
I really appreciate her involvement in this book. I'm also grateful to Andrea Warner for her book
Buffy Sainte-Marie: The Authorized Biography (Greystone Books, 2018).

Thanks also to Suzanne Methot for her review and to Dr. Kevin Lewis
for his guidance on nêhiyawêwin (Cree) language use.

Many thanks to bob and MJ and Zoe and Genevieve for their support of yet another book.
Thanks for all you do to help others.

Thanks always to Douglas and John. And many thanks to Paul who, like Buffy, does so much to
make the world a better place.

Scholastic Canada Ltd.
604 King Street West, Toronto, Ontario M5V 1E1, Canada

Scholastic Inc.
557 Broadway, New York, NY 10012, USA

Scholastic Australia Pty Limited
PO Box 579, Gosford, NSW 2250, Australia

Scholastic New Zealand Limited
Private Bag 94407, Botany, Manukau 2163, New Zealand

Scholastic Children's Books
Euston House, 24 Eversholt Street, London NW1 1DB, UK

www.scholastic.ca

The illustrations were created using a blend of digital tools with traditional media.
Sketches were created with a Wacom tablet and Photoshop, then traced onto watercolour paper,
where colour and texture were added using gouache and watercolour paints.
Ink was used to add the black line to finish the art.

Photos ©: cover, 1 speech balloon: fatmayilmaz/Getty Images; 30 left: Canada Post
© 2021; 30 right: David Gahr/Getty Images; 31 left: Phil Hossack/Free Press; 31 right:
Dustin Rabin. All other stock images © Getty Images.

Library and Archives Canada Cataloguing in Publication
Title: Meet Buffy Sainte-Marie / Elizabeth MacLeod ; illustrated by Mike Deas.
Names: MacLeod, Elizabeth, author. | Deas, Mike, 1982- illustrator.
Description: Series statement: Scholastic Canada biography
Identifiers: Canadiana 20220395470 | ISBN 9781443196123 (hardcover) |
ISBN 9781443196116 (softcover)
Subjects: LCSH: Sainte-Marie, Buffy—Juvenile literature | LCSH: Musicians
—Canada—Biography—Juvenile literature. | LCSH: Singers—Canada
—Biography—Juvenile literature. | LCSH: Composers—Canada—Biography
—Juvenile literature. | LCSH: Cree Indians—Canada—Biography
—Juvenile literature. | LCGFT: Biographies.
Classification: LCC ML420.S155 M33 2023 | DDC j782.42164092—dc23

6 5 4 3 2 1   Printed in China 62   23 24 25 26 27